High School Fundraising Secrets

High School Fundraising Secrets

ISBN: 1449999514
EAN-13: 9781449999513

Printed in the United States of America

First Printing February, 2010.

Acknowledgements

Thanks to my fellow teachers all over the world who encourage the intellect, spirit, and emotional growth of our fellow human beings. You are my inspiration for writing this book.

Thanks to the wonderful students that I teach every day. It is an honor to be your teacher.

And thanks, Dave Thomas, for teaching me that you can be proud to pass the hat for a good cause. Real proud.

A special note from the author

Thanks for purchasing my book. I wish you the very best and look forward to hearing your success story at info@highschoolfundraisingsecrets.com.

There are tons of websites out there promising big returns on fundraisers – but not all of them speak the truth. This is the real deal. I've tried almost all of this stuff, and I'm eager to share what I've learned with you.

Please know that I've intentionally tried to stay pretty vendor-neutral in this book. There are two reasons for that. First, I don't want you to think that someone has paid me to advertise their company or services. (They haven't.) Second, I usually go with the company that can offer me the best deal – even if I've worked with them before.

I've purposefully written the book in a conversational manner. If I had a choice between following "accepted grammar rules" and making the text flow, I went with flow. I want this to be a no-nonsense experience for you. Read this as if the two of us are having a cup of coffee in the teacher's cafeteria. I'm just sharing my thoughts, experiences, and knowledge in fundraising with you.

Thanks, and good luck with your fundraiser!

Introduction

This guide is meant for anyone trying to raise funds for a specific group of people or event. Your fundraiser can benefit a local food pantry that needs donations, a football team that needs new uniforms, students going on an educational trip, or maybe you're trying to replace an outdated computer lab.

Regardless of why you're raising money, these are all real techniques that I've used successfully for almost ten years. Some may work better than others, but the underlying principals are the same.

When I'm trying to raise a substantial amount of money, my basic process looks something like this:

1. Develop a coalition
2. Set a goal
3. Ask for donations
4. Sell things
5. Get creative

That basic formula has been the secret to my success. Let's get started. The first thing that you'll need with any successful fundraiser is a **coalition**.

Chapter 1 - Planning a coalition

When faced with a large task, the more people you have working on it, the more you can accomplish. Think about it – a moving company won't show up with just one or two workers to move a four bedroom house. They're going to arrive with an army of people. So should you. This is a war! You're the commander-in-chief, and you need to assemble your army to lead the charge. I don't care if you're trying to raise $500 or $50,000. A coalition will get more accomplished than you will acting on your own.

This is where most student organizations fall short – the fundraising team is comprised of a teacher, some students, maybe some parents... and that's it. Those people are very important parts of the operation, but if that's all you have, you're missing several key players. So let's assemble your army. Let's go over everyone that you should have on your team.

#1: Student volunteers and organizations

Most of the time, this is the easiest group to get motivated and working for you and your cause. Regardless of your status within the school – whether you're a teacher, counselor, social worker, or staff member – my guess is that you already have a core group of students that will follow your every move, do anything you ask of them, with the fundraiser. Teachers, maybe these are the students that stay after school and ask lots of questions in class. Or maybe they're not. After a fundraiser, sometimes I'll notice that the best student workers were the ones that didn't necessarily do well in my class. Sometimes I'll have an academically lackluster student volunteer to help me, and a funny thing happens: That student pays much better attention in class after they've spent some time on a project that's not entirely class-related. Once the student gets to know you on a more personal level, and sees your passion for helping students succeed, those uninspired students start to transform into active learners. I know that doesn't make you any money, but it's a great teaching experience.

Many times, the purpose of a fundraiser is to support a particular group of students – the football team, the cheerleaders, the chess team, etc. These students are, of course, the beneficiaries of all the donations, and will be eager to help with the fundraiser. Don't be afraid to partner with other clubs and organizations. They are not your competition. There is indeed strength in numbers during a fundraiser. If the chess team has 15 members and the fashion club has 15 members, there's no reason why these two teams can't partner up. Having 30 students sell a product instead of just 15 greatly increases the number of students – and parents – that you can reach.

Actively search for other clubs and organizations that are in need of a fundraiser, or one that has a size similar to your own. Of course, if you're in charge of 100 football players, you may not need a "partner organization" to sell products with, but it doesn't hurt to consider it.

#2: Past graduates

Graduates of the school that have gone on to bigger things often feel a sense of responsibility to help their alma matter out a bit. Perhaps your school has an online alumni listing, or a sheet of retired teachers and their addresses. Since these people already have ties to the school, getting them to donate a mere $5 to $10 for your event isn't that hard... and most fundraiser organizers won't bother to take the time to contact these people. But you're different. Your fundraiser is a big deal. (Even if it may not seem like it, approach your fundraiser as if it will be a defining moment in your career. It just might end up being one.)

A short postcard or letter to graduates explaining your cause, your fundraiser, and a reference to the "school's family" often hits home. (Say your school name is Springfield South. In the letter, mention that you are "seeking support from our Springfield South family.") Ask for $5 to $10 and you'll often get $20 or more.

#3: Local school administration

Your local school administration is another ally that you need to get on-board. I know that some school administrations are easier to work with than others, and that some school administrations are... less than approachable, depending on your district. I have always had the good fortune of working for people whom I respected, and I got support and respect in return. My principal was always willing to let us try new things, as long as it didn't put us in a precarious legal position. For example, we always had to make sure food sales were handled in a sanitary manner, and we had to comply with local ordinance / code (our town wouldn't let us sell 50/50 "split the pot" fundraiser tickets without a permit, for example).

School administration exists for reasons like this. If they say that you can't do a fundraiser, then you can't do a fundraiser. It might be a good idea to check with your building principal before advertising an event. This gives your principal a heads-up (which they'll appreciate, since they like to know what's going on in their building) and allows them to throw out a red flag if they know of any issues that might arise. (Which is *good*, since you don't want to get in any legal trouble or step on the toes of powerful people.)

Most of the time, I'm of the school of thought that says, "It's easier to ask forgiveness than to ask permission." But with fundraising, I put that aside and ask first, and suggest that you do the same.

#4: District administration

I know that some districts are larger than others, and districts with more than a few schools sometimes lose the possibility of personally knowing the superintendent or the assistant superintendents. But these people have valuable links to the community and board of education that can't be overlooked. If you're selling something cute (like stuffed animals or little stocking stuffers during the holidays), take a trip to the district administrative office. When you arrive, explain to the secretaries what you're selling and who it benefits. Most of the time, they're willing to buy one because they have a nephew / niece / grandson / cousin / etc. that would just adore one of them. More than that, when "the boss" asks about the little stuffed pumpkin or elf creature that their assistant has displayed on his / her desk, the assistants will be able to do some further selling for you.

If an assistant or secretary goes out of their way to help you, be sure to thank them appropriately. Remember that secretaries do talk to each other – and their boss – about the people that come into the office.

#5: A few other teachers

Unless you're brand-new to the school district, you've got some allies in your fellow faculty members. So use them. And if you are new to the school, recruit other first-year teachers to help.   You'll make a name for yourselves together. Be careful about who you pick as a fundraising partner – while it may seem like a good idea to recruit teachers from your own department or group, ask yourself if they have something meaningful to contribute to your fundraiser. There's nothing worse than one person pulling all the weight.   Find someone to work with that will contribute as much to the cause as you will.

#6: Parents

I usually don't specifically involve parents in my fundraising strategies, because I don't have ultra-supportive parents in my school. At least, not as supportive as I see them from other schools. It's not because our parents don't love their kids as much. Far from it. It's because I work in a community where both parents have to work for the family to live comfortably. Maybe that's true for your area, or maybe not. Regardless, if you have a PTA that meets regularly, it might be a good partnership opportunity. PTA moms and dads are usually very involved with the school and will contribute to a fundraiser that seems worthy. Get the PTA president on your side, and you can probably advertise for free in the next PTA newsletter that goes home to all the other supportive PTA moms and dads.

#7: Local Government

Local government is one of the most overlooked sources of fundraising revenue. This takes more time and energy than some of the normal fundraising methods, but it's also one of the most rewarding.

First of all, don't be intimidated by going into the mayor's office. (Yeah, that's right, you're going to have to go and meet the mayor.) Most mayors have a genuine desire to help their constituents, and schools are especially good P.R. opportunities. Even if the mayor's office can't help you directly, they can be invaluable links to other local organizations and the people within them. At the very least, if the town's donation budget is exhausted, they can help spread the word.

And right now, you might be thinking, "Yeah, right. Like the mayor is going to help us raise money for the math team, or the science fair, or send the cheerleaders to camp." You'd be surprised – I always hear from our Board of Education and from local officials that they spend most of their time in dry, stale meetings, trying to work with people that can be less than pleasurable. Meeting a group of young, promising students with broad smiles is often the highlight of their week. It's even more likely that your local government offices will help you if your group is providing a "community service" – like raising money for S.A.D.D. (Students Against Drunk Driving), Operation Snow-ball (which promotes a drug-free environment), or a local food drive. Debate teams, chess teams, and any other type of "knowledge" competition brings academic honor to the local school and community. Mayors love to brag about the quality of their local high school, and will be eager to help you in this endeavor.

Now, some pointers:

First, assistants and other "secretaries" to the mayor are meant to screen out telemarketers and people that will be wasting the mayor's valuable time. It helps to already be familiar with the name of this person, which you can likely get through the school principal's or superintendent's office. Of course, these two offices talk to each other occasionally. If you're on really good terms with your secretaries (and you should be, as mentioned previously), then TELL THEM about your project and how you plan to talk to the mayor's office. They will be helpful with providing you with their contact information.

One of the titles that I've found to be useful in every town is the "Director of Human Resources." Why? They know EVERYBODY. Human Resources is in charge of hiring, and most of the time, have at least some kind of hand in the town's public relations. I found many connections to local Bingo Halls, Kiwanis groups, and other people that otherwise might not have listened to my request for funding... but did because I went through the town's Director of Human Resources. Someone in your school district might already know who this is. If not, research it on the web. Every town has a website, so use it to learn the names of important people that you don't already know.

This can become harder if you're in a huge metropolitan area – i.e. in the heart of L.A., New York, Chicago, etc. Getting into the mayor's office in Los Angeles is much more difficult than a mayor of a nearby suburb. Possible, but difficult. In this case, use other local government officials to help you in. Aldermen, state representatives, state senators, national representatives, etc. can help you get a foot in the door, if you plead your case.

#8: Local Businesses

Depending on your fundraising strategy, some local businesses will be more than happy to chip in. Corporate sponsorships can provide lots of money. Often times, if you agree to promote a business among the staff or forward that business' contact information to your school paper, you can get a small check without much trouble at all. Concentrate on asking for funds from businesses that your town is known for, if possible. If you're in a manufacturing town, then hit every manufacturer through the local Chamber of Commerce. Ask local fast food establishments for a small donation. (They might try to get you to do a profit-sharing night. More on that later...) Tell them that at every basketball game, football game, or after every math team meeting, that you'll announce to the crowd, or the students, that the local McDonalds on Main Street is a great partner to work with, and that the season couldn't have been a success without their help. Offer to have the game's announcer advertise a special, which could bring a significant "after the game" crowd. (Say that your Local Dairy Queen agrees to a 99 cent ice cream promotion that you will advertise to the basketball fans during the game. There will be plenty more "side business" as a result of the promotion, and any good DQ manager will know that.)

If you're fundraising to make prom more affordable, ask local florists and limo companies to offer you a free corsage or 3 hours of limo service that you can raffle off and use the profits toward your event. Think about what your goals are for this fundraiser and use that to FOCUS on local businesses.

Assembled and ready to depart!

So that's your coalition. You've got students, teachers, parents, building administration, community and local government leaders, and you. Now that your army is assembled, it's time to start fundraising. At this point, if you have and know your specific goal, it might be prudent to start out by asking everyone on your team for donations – and while you're waiting for them to come in, advertise your goals. We'll talk about both of these topics in chapters 2 and 3.

Chapter 2 – The Power of Donations

Ah, the power of donations. Let me tell you a success story – how I raised over $12,000 without personally selling a thing.

I was given the task by our school of planning activities for a week that would be filled with anti-drug / anti-alcohol messages but would also emphasize positive decision making and promote a friendly school culture. I was given a mere $750 to start out with – that was it. That was my budget. Some of the events that the weeklong event included:

- An all-school speaker that would address the entire student body on one of the above topics
- A dance for the students, to show that they could have a good time without using drugs or alcohol
- Other small sessions throughout the week consisting of many speakers introducing a variety of topics.

After looking at the budget, I knew I needed funds fast. I did some research in my metropolitan area and found that a GOOD all-school speaker costs around $3,000 and I only had a quarter of that. And I wanted more than a dance. Many students, especially at the high school level, are not entirely comfortable with dating the opposite sex. What I wanted was a good time for EVERY student… even those that didn't like to dance. To that end, I decided to hire an inflatable entertainment company to come out and blow up an inflatable obstacle course, a "bungee run," inflatable boxing, and more. I wanted to have a corner dedicated to "Guitar Hero" and "Dance Dance Revolution" contests. I wanted a good DJ to act as Master of Ceremonies for the night. I wanted to advertise "all you can eat pizza" to draw the student population in. The problem: All of this costs money.

My first step was to ask our school administration for additional funds. I was told that this was the most that they could allocate for this school year, but that additional funding *might* be possible. I raised concerns that I would not be able to do much without some fundraising and so I got the blessing of my school to do so.

I inquired in our district administration office about the possibility of using Title IV money for this. There are Federal grants available for anti-drug programs at schools. As long as we could show that we were fostering a "safe" school environment (We were!) then we were eligible for that money. I was told that I could apply for funds through one of our district superintendents. After a few hours of inquiries, a form, and a little persistence, I was awarded $2,000 for the program.

My next step was to approach local government offices. My school served several communities, and I started with the mayor's office in each. My success varied from town to town. One mayor never returned my phone calls and letters, and was never in the office when I dropped by to ask for an appointment. Another mayor sent me $50, another sent me $100. While the local police departments

13

couldn't allocate funds, one did agree to come by with a free "drug dog" presentation and talk to the students about the capabilities of the dogs, some of the things they found at traffic stops, when they arrested people, and to answer any questions the students might have. I thought that it would be great for our students to meet the local police BEFORE they got stopped for a traffic violation, so that they knew the local police were just looking out for them. This was essentially a free speaker, which was great, since it would lower the total amount I needed to raise. The local fire department offered the use of their facilities for a car wash fundraiser, and all we'd have to do is get some students to volunteer. The problem was that my event was in March, and January / February are cold months for that kind of event. I resolved to try it out early in the next academic year.

One of the local governments was extremely generous. I approached the mayor's office and asked to present my case to the local town officials at a town hall meeting. The mayor's office was delighted to help, especially since the mayor himself was a graduate of our school district. After pleading my case, the mayor's office presented me with a check for $3,300. I was ecstatic. I now had enough money to cover our all-school speaker, the inflatable games for the party (which cost $2,000, despite my excellent bargaining skills), and the DJ. (Our school administration had ties with another past graduate of the school, who ran a small DJ setup on the side for extra cash. He was happy to DJ the party for $325 and played good music that the students really enjoyed.)

Still unsatisfied, I knew that pizza and soda would cost a bundle if I paid for it outright. I explained to local pizzerias what I was doing and many were eager to help. Some offered pizza at cost, some offered free pizza if I would send someone to pick it up, and some offered to deliver 5 free pizzas on the night of the event. I planned on 500 students attending the event, and "All you can Eat" pizza for all of them cost me only $300. In return, I proudly displayed menus of the pizzerias that donated, which cost me nothing. This saved me a bundle. I asked one of our local food stores to donate a gift card, which I used to purchase bottled water, and asked a local soda distributor to donate some soda cases to us. Best of all, I stumbled upon another school graduate that owned a business that sold and rented juicer machines. (You add syrup and water in a specific concentration to come up with fruit punch, lemonade, etc. The juicers simply mix and chill the product.) He donated the use of these machines and several gallons of the syrup. We ended up having enough refreshment for all of the students, volunteers, and DJ. If I would have paid retail for the beverage items alone, it would have cost me well over $700. With an event like this, saving money is essentially the same thing as raising money. I felt like I was on a roll, and could have stopped there if I wanted to, but I still had to plan for the costs of "breakout" speakers throughout the week.

I looked up "Chamber of Commerce" along with our city name in Google and sent a mass mailing out with school-provided postage. (The postage was discounted, because I pre-sorted the letters and sent it out in our "non-profit" envelopes.) I sent letters to over 250 companies and organizations, and about 12 responded with various amounts.

Twelve respondents doesn't seem like a whole lot – especially when you've sent out 250 letters! But, don't be discouraged. Twelve people donating around $100 each can give you a quick $1,200. I ended up with more than that – but before I tell you my total from the mailings, there are some "mass mailing" secrets that I have learned after years of doing this:

First, most modern word processors know how to do something called a "mail merge." This is where you take a list of businesses in a spreadsheet or database and combine them with a form letter to give the illusion of a personalized letter. If you don't know how to use this feature, find someone that does, and learn how to use it! You'll be using it to print both letters and envelopes.

Advertisers that use the USPS make use of mail merge technology. When you get "junk mail" at home, and it's addressed to "Dear Occupant," chances are good that you'll throw it away without much thought. On the other hand, something that has your name on it and the return address of your old high school is probably something that you'd open.

Second, ask for a specific amount – and don't be shy. Because of the large amount of money I had to raise, I asked for $250 in the initial mailing. Some sent $100, some went beyond what I asked for and sent $500. I sent another round of letters out after I worked the mayor's office at one of the local municipalities for some phone numbers and contact information for our local Kiwanis, trustees, Bingo Hall, and other organizations that might be willing to help us. My grand total for businesses ended up at just over $4,500. I was astounded at the generosity of our community. $4,500 just by sending out letters and asking for help!

My final step in this massive fundraiser was to recruit another teacher to do a fundraiser in his class to help us out and donate the profits to my event. I didn't personally have the time to coordinate and launch a product-based fundraiser, but he worked it into his normal daily classroom activities. He used the event to teach students marketing skills, computer desktop publishing skills, balance sheets, profit margins, and a wide variety of other topics. He had a connection with a local McDonald's restaurant and another at Subway Sandwiches. The local franchises sold us sandwiches at cost, and he sold them with his class during lunch periods to our hungry students, which was a welcome change of pace from the standard cafeteria fare. We were sure to promote it heavily, and asked the cafeteria staff to prepare for somewhat slower than usual business on that day. His net income from that event was over $600, which he generously donated to my cause. I didn't have to sell anything – I was just there watching, and the students did all the work. It was great! If your school has a marketing or business class, see if they'll join your coalition in exchange for a small percentage of the profits, free sandwiches, etc.

That event pushed my total to just over $12,000! We used the extra money to bring in a wide variety of other speakers, purchase anti-drug banners, buy some "Buckle up!" stickers, and get some sandwiches for our party as a "healthy" option for those that didn't really want pizza.

Here's my little income statement:

Amount raised or saved:	How we got it:
$750	School donation as start-up money
$2,000	Title IV money
$3,450	Local governments
$250	Free event speaker
$4,500	Local businesses
$600	Having a partner sell food at lunch
$300	Savings from pizza discounts
$700	Savings in beverage purchases
Over $12,000	**TOTAL**

So what did I do for this $12,000? I attended meetings, made phone calls and wrote letters. Notice that the food fundraiser actually ended up being unnecessary and was less than 5% of my total income. We had plenty of room in the budget to spare, but once other teachers heard that I was doing fundraising in record amounts, they were eager to get in on the success story and contribute to my cause. I welcomed donations from the teachers that wanted to help – from selling food at lunch to donating small amounts – and used that money for stickers, drug-free ribbons, and other items that helped me promote the week. We used the surplus during the following year, when the economy started to falter nation-wide, and donations were less than what they were in the past.

Take a look at your coalition roster again. (See the first chapter of this book.) Who did we <u>directly</u> use?

- ✓ Student volunteers
- ✓ Local school administration
- ✓ District administration
- ✓ Other teachers
- ✗ Parents
- ✓ Local Government
- ✓ Local Businesses
- ✓ Personal Contacts and Past Graduates

See what I mean about the whole coalition thing? That was a TEAM effort – and if you're reading this book, you're the project manager (or someone close to the project manager). Sometimes all you have to do is coordinate the troops and let them go to work. Just be sure that they have a goal in mind as they're working. Need help with that? Read Chapter 3.

Chapter 3 – Setting and achieving goals

Setting a goal for your troops to work towards is important. I could, but won't, quote multiple studies from a wide variety of researchers that say *goal setting is important and results in great success.*

I like to set goals AFTER my donations come in, because that's the amount of money that I really have to work hard for. Setting a goal is usually pretty easy. Most fundraisers have a specific amount of money that they'd like to raise. For example, I knew in the chapter two success story, that I'd have to raise at least $5,000 to get my event off the ground. Set your goal high (my goal was $10,000) but within reason. I like to set timeframes for my goal, too. "By March 1st, I'd like to have over $10,000 in the bank." But here's a little secret, just between you and me:

Ready?

It's okay if you don't reach your entire fundraising goal.

Go ahead and re-read the line above. I'll wait.

Now, before you throw this book down on the ground in disgust (or shut off that digital reader of yours), hear me out. Let's say your goal is to raise $10,000 for breast cancer awareness. You set up an elaborate armada to assist you, and have the coolest ideas ever. In the end, you only raise $7,350 for cancer research. Think about that for a minute – the press release that you send out won't say "High School

Group fails to reach its goal!" It'll say "Totally Awesome Fundraising donates thousands of dollars to the fight against cancer!" Songs will be written about your fundraiser, and the school will erect a golden statue of your likeness near the front entrance! Well, maybe it won't go quite that far... but you get the idea.

Even if you're raising money for new football team uniforms, it's possible to go to the sports apparel store and say, "Listen, I've done as much fundraising as I can possibly do. This is for the *kids*. Can't we make a deal here?" I'd be willing to bet that they'd negotiate down a price, at least somewhat. And if they don't, you can return to your administration, saying "Look, I tried my hardest. I know you've got some kind of budget money somewhere. This is for our *kids*. Can't we make a deal here?"

So, coming close to a goal is usually just as good as meeting it. And if you follow the tips in this guide, I'll bet that you make a heck of a dent in whatever fundraising goal you have before you.

The key to goals is making sure your entire school population and community know what they are, and how you're doing with them. There are a variety of ways to do this.

Student Bulletins

Every school has a daily bulletin, right? Some schools announce them, some broadcast them over the in-house TV system, some schools put them into paper format. Whatever your school does, take advantage of it to advertise your goal. You can either have the students announce that you are 2 weeks into your fundraiser and halfway to your goal... or get on the PA system personally and plead for help. (Hint: <u>Write down what you're going to say</u> before you do this. Even the most outgoing teachers stumble the first couple of times they make an announcement on the PA system.)

Thermometers

You've seen these, right? I see one all the time for my local United Way® branch when they need to raise funds. They're popular and easy to understand. Step One: Find a high-visibility area. This could be the cafeteria, main entrance to your school, computer lab, library, or all four of these locations. Step Two: Go online and find a template for a blank fundraising thermometer. At the time of this writing, there are several that appear towards the top of the rankings in a very popular search engine. Step Three: Fill in the thermometer with red marker every time you get a major donation, or at least once per week. Have some students help you to keep it as current as possible.

Alternatively, there are online fundraising thermometers. It wouldn't be hard to bam up a quick webpage (Find your high school's webmaster, or a web design class in need of an extra credit project) that shows your progress over time. It's a great way to spread the word – attach the site to

Facebook®, MySpace® and other social networking sites, and you've got lots of hits (translated: *awareness*), real fast.

School Marquee

Some schools have electronic marquee signs that can be programmed to display a variety of messages. If your school has one, ask the person in charge if you can have a quick "blurb" on there. If not, you can still ask to have the old-fashioned letters advertise your event, particularly during a high-traffic night like parent-teacher conferences or open house.

If for whatever reason your school has a policy against letting teachers advertise their causes on the marquee, be sure to leave flyers in high-traffic areas of the school during the all-school events like open house. Take advantage of high-visibility situations.

Word of Mouth

Another quick success story: Not long ago, one of my student organizations organized a local food and clothing drive during the holiday season. We didn't form a huge coalition or a massive plea for help to our local partners, though we could have. It was a hard year economically in our district, and we wanted to keep our message simple: "Please donate what you can, and it will help local area families in need."

That was it – that was our message. We found two food pantries that needed food and another organization that asked for everything from winter coats to jeans to t-shirts and yes, even socks. They would take everything that we'd bring to them and put the items to good use.

We had done similar drives in past years, so the annual event was well-known to most of the faculty, students, and staff. As a school, we usually donated between 7,000 to 9,000 items to charity. As soon as the event started, I realized that donations would be hard to come by. Most of the donations that initially came in were clothing. A few bags of canned goods would come in occasionally, or a box of ramen noodle soup would appear in the donation area. I feared that the two food pantries that came to rely on large donations from my school might not get much at all this year. As the fundraiser entered its final week, I saw a definite lack of progress and for the first time in my teaching career, was genuinely worried about the families receiving the aid. I stayed up late for a few nights figuring out how much money I could share from my personal budget to fund a trip to the grocery store.

Some students wanted to help but didn't want to go through the trouble of hauling cans from the grocery store into the classroom. So, our organization accepted monetary donations and I offered to match any monetary donation from my students. After about a week, I had a total of $160 and went to a local discount grocery store for cans of food, pasta, and other basic household staples. (After reading the last chapter, $160 may not sound like much, but it can actually buy a lot of food.) I filled a huge cart with cartons of macaroni, instant potatoes, soups, stews, stuffings, and vegetables. As I entered the checkout line, other people began to stare at my overfilled cart. (Perhaps they were apprehensive about waiting in line, since there was only one cashier on duty.) There was a young couple behind me in line that started to mumble. The whispering started:

"I'll bet he owns a restaurant!"

"Nah. He has a big family to feed."

"Are you kidding? He's probably just stocking up."

I wanted to turn around and say, "I can <u>hear</u> you. You're only about six feet away from me!" when one of them finally hit it.

"Either that, or it's for a food shelter."

At that point, I turned around and said, "Actually, it is." They asked me which one and I simply said, "It's for a town that I teach in. We're doing a food drive." The young woman looked at the man, then pulled out a $5 bill from her purse and asked if she could help pay for some of the groceries, and apologized that it wasn't much. I thanked her and went to get another case of canned vegetables. The people behind her must've felt awful, because they too started to reach for their wallets. They gave me $3, the people behind them, $10. I was amazed that the people I had inconvenienced with a long checkout line were so willing to help a perfect stranger like me. After I made it through the checkout line, I glanced back and waved at the kind folks that helped me, and found that I had to struggle to keep my composure.

The next day, my superintendent asked me how our annual drive was going. I told her that we were struggling, and the story from the day before. She must've made a heck of a sales pitch for me, because at the end of the day, I had over $600 in personal donations from our superintendents and their support staff of secretaries. It was such a great feeling to go back to our local food pantries and say, "Tell me what you still need, and I'll do my best to fill it."

Call it luck if you want to, but I see it as "Word of Mouth." Tell people what you're doing. If I hadn't turned around in the grocery store, I never would have seen such an act of generosity. If I hadn't relayed that heart-warming story to my administration, I probably wouldn't have had over $600 to go shopping with the next day. Tell people how things are going, advertise your progress towards your goals, and eventually, good things will come your way.

Before we move on to the next chapter, I want to remind you that schools (in my state) are tax exempt for club purchases. As this was actually a purchase from my student organization, it was considered to be tax-free. It never hurts to keep a copy of your district's sales tax letter on file from the appropriate office. The tax savings allowed us to purchase more food and help more people – which is what this fundraiser was all about.

Chapter 4 – Selling traditional stuff

All right. You've begged and pleaded with the help of your coalition, and have written more letters than you ever thought possible. You've set your goal and are still coming up short. You finally realize that you're going to have to offer something for sale the next time that you pass the hat around for your cause. Selling stuff is what most people call a "traditional" fundraiser. There are advantages and disadvantages to these events, but when donations run dry, this is your next best strategy of attack.

Negotiate!

Before we proceed, I need to tell you that, regardless of what you decide to sell, NEGOTIATE before you order it. This can be intimidating to some people, but even little things can add up. If you're ordering something as simple as pizza slices, and the pizzeria total comes out to $550, explain to the order taker that it's for a school fundraiser, and that your budget is only $500. Or, if you're ordering from a T-shirt company, ask if they can "comp" the shipping charges because it's for a school. Of course, mention to the vendor that if the fundraiser is successful, you'll be ordering more in the future. As you're negotiating, as previously mentioned, don't forget to check that the final order is tax exempt.

If you're not in a hurry to buy, and really want to earn some extra dollars on the project, put on your best poker face. If you're calling a company to negotiate down a price, and the person on the other end isn't budging, you can always say something like, "Well, thanks for your help, Tom. The grand total of $589 is just over my budget right now. I'll be calling some other folks for some quotations. You have my name and number – maybe you can talk to your manager for me, and tell him that if you can meet that $500 budget limit of mine, we'd have a deal." Promptly end the call, and sometimes, within an hour or two, you have the sales rep back on the phone, eager to take your $500. Congratulations. You've just earned $89 on your project.

So what are the traditional items to sell?

Candy

Selling candy is perhaps the most common school fundraising strategy, and with good reason. Most people like candy, it's an easy product to sell that everyone's familiar with, it's cheap for the purchaser (usually $1) when compared with other products, and the transaction occurs right away. There's no complex order/fulfillment process, and you can sell it almost anywhere. The profit margin is decent, and you can either go through an official company (that will give you pre-mixed candy bars from Nestle®, Hershey®, etc. with an official-looking box), or you can go to a local warehouse club and purchase candy yourself in bulk. The official company obviously gives your fundraiser a degree of professionalism and credibility, but if you don't want to deal with getting a school check or want to get started immediately, then the second option may be best for you.

If you've never tried a candy sale before, here are some things you need to think about:

First, how will you get the up-front money to pay for the initial candy? Sometimes, it may be necessary to make the purchase on a personal credit card. The nice thing about going through a professional company (instead of buying it at a warehouse club) is that they're used to this problem. They'll front you the candy and expect payment within 2 or 3 weeks. They also know you're tax exempt and how to deal with it. Go through a local warehouse and you'll have to put the money up yourself, and deal with the tax exemption thing.

Second, once you have a big pile of candy to sell, how are you going to track each seller's / student's progress? A program like Microsoft Excel can help you with this, but it really is best to say something like, "Here's 20 candy bars. You need to pay me $20 after you sell them and I'll give you another 12/24/36/whatever." Some students will invariably sell faster than others, so be prepared for one student to sell 50 candy bars while another is trying to sell 20. It's very easy to forget to record money coming in and out during the school day, and it's important to know how much you have coming in and how much product is still out there. Be prepared for the occasional student to take their 20 initial bars, and say something like "I lost the candy bars" or "My mom took them to work and never paid me the money for them." You have the option, of course, of asking the students to pay back the cost of the candy (sometimes things DO happen), or simply forgive the debt, trusting them with less candy to sell in the future.

Keeping track of where all the product and money is, will be much harder than you'd think, and it's helpful to have another teacher help you with this. Otherwise, students tend to "forget" to pay you, and your profit margins get killed. You end up making a few hundred bucks after selling cases and cases of candy. Lots of work, not a whole lot of gain.

Most faculty and staff are good about the "honor system." If your school allows it, place a small box of assorted candy with a sign that says, "French Club fundraiser - $1 each" in strategic places like the copy room, mail room, etc. It'll be better-received if your little sign is professional. Don't hand-write it on a scratch sheet of copy paper. Take the time in Microsoft Word to bam up a professional little sign and print it out on nice, thick paper. The people around you will appreciate your professionalism and classiness.

Are there other things you can do with candy? Sure – look for opportunities to promote your sale. Most high schools have some kind of theater department. Ask the current production coordinator if your group can sell intermission snacks, and offer a percentage of the profits to them in return if you meet resistance.

If you're not friendly with the school's cafeteria personnel, get to know them. I've found that some of my best allies during fundraisers are usually the workers in the cafeteria. Not only will they agree to stop selling candy for a few days (since I'm selling it), but they'll usually buy some in return, especially if it's unique to your cause.

What makes something a "unique" candy fundraiser? Have the type of candy sold match your group's purpose. For example, a technology or computer club could sell "Nerd Ropes®" because most people think of nerds as people with thick, taped glasses. Seems to fit the phrase "computer club," doesn't it? Go and get some cheap plastic nerd glasses and have everybody that's selling candy put on a pair for the day to promote the fundraiser. It's different. It's fresh. It's catchy. It's not the boring and tired sales phrase, "Wanna buy a chocolate bar?" Come up with a similar strategy for your group.

T-shirts

First of all, T-shirts are generally not good money makers. Some people sell T-shirts at a small profit, but this is a very difficult fundraiser to get a decent profit from. Let's be honest – you're not going to want to charge people more than $10 for a T-shirt... because many people just won't pay it, even if it's got a clever logo or saying on it. For some students, $10 can pay for an entire WEEK's worth of lunches.

Second, T-shirt companies can be hard to handle. You've got to work with them to get the artwork just right, make sure the text and spelling is perfect, decide on one or two colors, etc. ALWAYS GET A PROOF (sample) from the company. I have heard many stories from many teachers about how they "trusted" a T-shirt company without seeing an example of the final product, and the shirts were nothing like what they had envisioned. If the company won't do this for you, then you don't want to be doing business with them. Find another vendor – either with a physical location, or an online one – that will.

As I said, profits can be a tricky thing. T-shirt companies may want to CHARGE you $10 per shirt. Net profit to you: nothing. Of course, you'll have to negotiate, but perhaps you can get the shirts down to $7 each. Recognize that the T-shirt company is in business to make a profit, and meet them somewhere in the middle. If you make $3 per shirt and sell 100 shirts, you take in $300. That's not a bad profit margin, but not a huge one, either. Remember that everything helps. If the T-shirt thing takes 2 or 3 weeks from start to finish, then that's still $300 that you didn't have before.

Finally, in my opinion, you can only really do one T-shirt sale per year. Most people have enough random T-shirts anyway, and after a while, they start to lose their appeal. I've been at my school district for quite a while now, and I'll occasionally help out the basketball, soccer, and softball teams with some kind of event. In return, the coaches give me a T-shirt, and so I have at least 20 shirts in my closet with my school name on them. I really don't need to spend ten bucks on another one from the Italian club, Snowboarding club, or Volleyball team. Make sure that you recognize that some of your faculty may be in a similar position. Target STUDENTS for T-Shirt sales, not faculty.

Bake sales

Bake sales are also tricky things. It requires a lot of student and parent involvement. Some customers might be reluctant to buy things made in other people's homes (and by looking at some of the cookies, perhaps rightly so...), while other homemade cookies look and taste great, and will sell out instantly. You know your school best, and what kind of bakery sells (or would sell) well.

Bake sales aren't exactly cash cows, and I personally don't like them because they require lots of parental involvement, which many schools don't have. In my high school, we shifted the emphasis on the event over to the students and turned a traditional fundraiser into one with a little more flair. It turned a conventional "ho-hum" bake sale into one of our school's most popular fundraisers. Let me tell you about it.

On select Friday mornings at about 7:00am, the foods classes in the high school offer coffee, cappuccinos, lattes, fruit smoothies, hot chocolate, chocolate covered pretzel bags, rice krispy treats, and all kinds of other delicious goodies. Imagine music with a Starbucks® kind of beat playing, and student servers in black barista-style aprons. The teachers and students really enjoy the event, and it kicks off the day right. It runs for half an hour right before we start classes, and is most successful the day before a spring break, Thanksgiving holiday, three-day weekend, etc. Coffee beverages sell for about $1, fruit smoothies sell for $2, and most baked goods are 75 cents to one dollar. The treats are affordable for customers, and when done *en masse*, it generates a decent chunk of money. Partner up with your local foods class. This is a great opportunity for the foods classes to show off their skills and get some real-world serving experience. To get in on a portion of the profits, offer to do all the grunt-work: Advertising within the school, running the cash register, directing students to the lines, setting up tables, cleaning up dishes, etc. Then, split the profits. When you have an armada of student helpers, this event really is a lot of fun and the profits roll in fast. Let's say that you sell about 300 coffee drinks, 150 smoothies, and about 100 cookies and other baked goods. Add it up, and you've made almost $700 ($350 after you split the profits) for a single morning's work, minus the cost of the materials. (Your foods teachers might pick up the cost of the materials out of their department's budget, if you're lucky.)

This event will definitely become more successful with practice – but at the high school level, it pulls in significantly more than a traditional bake sale would.

If your school doesn't offer culinary elective options, and you're not the type to mix hot chocolate and coffee to make mochas, then get that coalition going again and ask some of the local coffee house baristas to come in and help you with the fundraiser. Get the town bakery to kick in some morning treats at cost. In a separate fundraiser, the Italian club in my school bought Italian cookies, cannoli, tiramisu, and other treats from the local bakery and added on a small profit margin to each product. They tasted great, it was a great Friday afternoon fundraiser, and you don't have to worry about baking cookies yourself.

Carwashes

It never fails – it's a warm, sunny, 80 degree day. As I'm driving past our local high school that's about two minutes from my house in the suburbs, I see a couple of students from either the local chapter of the National Honor Society or the local high school cheerleaders waving wildly at me with their homemade signs, advertising a carwash. For the first three years that I lived in my suburban home, I didn't stop once. I felt bad, but I was always on my way somewhere, dead tired from a long day, just didn't want to wait in line, or my car was actually already clean.

One June morning, I had the day to myself and was on the way to the grocery store with no particular timeline whatsoever. Sure enough, I was driving with the windows open and the radio jamming, and I could see the carwash signs ahead with huge arrows and students directing me to pull in. "What the heck," I thought, and pulled into the high school parking lot.

The school wasn't asking for any particular amount – but rather a donation to be used to fund the local NHS chapter. The students seemed nice, and as they were starting to spray my car with water and pull out the sponges, I found one of the people in charge, made a donation of $20, and started asking about the pros and cons of such an event, since I had never attempted one. Here's what he told me:

Car washes are a lot of fun, but can actually be <u>dangerous</u> on a hot day. Not only do you have the possibility of sunburn for students waving down cars driving by on a busy street, but you (as an adviser, coach, teacher, etc.) have the added responsibility of switching kids between the carwash station and the advertising station, making sure students have (and re-apply) sunscreen, and stay hydrated. Sunburn is annoying and painful, but dehydration is far more serious. Lose track of one fair-skinned student and you've got a case of severe sunburn and/or dehydration on your hands.

<u>Low participation rate</u> – Turns out most of the cars for this summer fundraiser that were being washed belonged to the family members of the students themselves... but the fundraiser was meant to help defray costs for the students and their families. The coach told me that the parents were okay with this, since the students were officially "working" for their club, but it seemed to me that the point of a fundraiser is to get external sources of money coming in.

Doing a good job – While you have no high-tech carwash equipment to help you here (a couple of buckets of soap, some sponges, and a long garden hose are probably all you have / can afford to get the job done), I was told that some people will actually bring back the car and tell them that the students "missed a spot" which gets other cars (that have been patiently waiting) upset. The students would happily re-wash, but after washing about ten cars, even the most dedicated student will miss spots and get tired under the hot sun.

Don't make it worse – the coach was quick to tell me that if I ever did a carwash fundraiser, that I should tell all the girls (and guys) to remove their rings and other jewelry before letting them near the sponges and dry-rags. There was an incident with this particular group where a girl had forgotten to do this... and completely covered the front end of an expensive car in ring scratches.

Medium to Low profit – I was told that if the carwash handled 100 cars, that they made 500 to 600 dollars, which is a good day's work, but by the time you factor in supplies, drying rags (which have to be continually re-dried unless you have a large supply), Gatorade for the group, sign materials, sunscreen, etc. the fundraiser becomes more of a bonding experience than a fundraiser. And maybe that's exactly what you need for your group.

So, you can give carwashes a try, but know that you need a lot of manpower (and luck – rainy days don't bring in much money) to pull this one off. The other problem is... when high schools are in session, it's usually pretty cool outside and your window of opportunity is limited. There are other ways to make money with cars, and I'll cover those in the next chapter.

There you have it – your traditional, all-American fundraisers. What do all of these traditional fundraisers have in common?

- Everyone does the same thing! If you work in a school, how many times have you seen students selling candy, or running a bake sale? You want to try to separate your group from others to gain visibility. The best way to do that is with unique fundraisers. Sell unique candy, put a new spin on the bake sale, and be creative to make your fundraiser successful.

- Lots of work. While you can't be afraid of a little hard work, candy sales, carwashes, bake sales, and T-shirt sales can take up a *lot* of time and work.

- Risk. Candy bars can melt, get lost or stolen, and attract pests if left out overnight. Carwashes need to be carefully monitored, and require good weather. T-shirts can be a headache, and if you order too many T-shirts, you'll actually have a loss on your hands... along with boxes of unsold shirts.

- Parental involvement. Great if you have a group of parents that have hours and hours of time to dedicate to your cause, but many people simply don't have this option.

- Low profit margins, if not done right. All it takes is a rainy day, a lost box or two of candy, T-shirts that won't sell, or a lousy bake sale turnout to eat up profit margins and make the fundraiser a wash.

Ready for some new ideas? Yeah. I thought so. Let's go!

Chapter Five – Selling New Stuff

In this chapter, we're going to talk about selling things that are outside the scope of traditional fundraisers. This is not a complete or comprehensive list, but it'll get your mind thinking outside the box. Once you have a product that people like, you'll have no problem selling it.

Flash drives

Nothing screams "We're tech-savvy" like flash drives. You can get these professionally customized for a relatively low price, and re-sell them with a $3 to $5 markup on them. They do sell themselves, for the most part. Just about everybody has used a USB flash drive / thumb drive / jump drive, and you can ALWAYS use another one to transfer files between two systems, or to carry an extra backup copy with you. The disadvantage of selling these: It's a lot of up-front money, especially if there's a minimum with the company you're buying from. Let's say you buy 100 pre-printed flash drives at $6 each. You need to put up $600 to place the initial order. Yes, you stand to make $400 if you sell them for $10, but it does require some initial investment. What's the solution if you're not comfortable with putting that much money on a credit card? Take pre-orders. Advertise the sale, and ask your faculty and students to email you or fill out an order form (this can be paper or online), and place payment in your mailbox. When you have sold 60 of your 100 drives, you can place your order and know that you won't lose money on the deal, and that everything else is pure profit. (And if you DON'T get 60 pre-orders relatively quickly, maybe it's a good thing that you didn't place that order... otherwise you'd be stuck with a lot of flash drives that you'd have to sell at a loss just to get some of your money back. Time to find another fundraiser.)

USB drives even come in pen form now. It's a pen with a base at the top that unscrews to magically reveal... a flash drive! Once students saw me use a USB pen drive that I got as a promotion from a trade show and offered to buy my freebie from me, I realized that I had a good potential fundraiser on my hands. Check online prices to see what kinds of deals you can swing.

Glow sticks

A quick order of glowsticks before the Homecoming Dance, football game, turnabout dance, etc. can make a quick night's profit. You can purchase 200 glow sticks at 40 cents each, sell them for $1 each, and you've made a quick $120. Not enough for an African safari, but that $120 is an easy two or three hours of work. Obviously, you'll need to make friends with whoever is in charge of the dance, as they might have the same idea. For example, if the French club is throwing a Mardi Gras dance, you might ask the French club sponsor if you can sell glow sticks during the evening. If you're lucky, you'll get a yes. Sometimes, though, the French club sponsor will realize, "Hey, I can do the same thing and funnel the profits to French club, instead!" and renege on the offer. In this case, your best bet is to give the French club a percentage of the profits — something like

25%. Mention that there's no work on their end, and at the end of the night, they get a few bucks to help cover the decorations, and party supplies. In my experience, other teachers are good at "sharing the wealth."

Glow sticks at football games work well in the fall. They can usually out-shine the lighting in the stands, and are fun for toddlers and teens alike. Certain glowsticks can be daisy-chained together to make necklaces from bracelets... or you can buy both small and large, charging an extra dollar for the larger size.

Taffy Apples

This has become one of my favorite fundraisers in the fall because it's unique, festive, and fun. It doesn't generate huge, enormous profits, but I have always had a good time with this one, and I think you will too. If you've never tried this before, research companies on the web and find one that will sell you taffy apples with and without nuts, and with Halloween-colored sprinkles. The profits are only about 40 cents per apple if you sell them at $1.00 each, but people generally like them and they are easy to sell because they're popular in the fall and not as common as candy.

I've used this Taffy Apple fundraiser many times before and it's most successful if you set a goal. In my school, we try to sell 1,000 Taffy Apples in 3 days. (We usually do this the three days before Thanksgiving weekend, since it's still "fall harvest" time and they make good treats for after-turkey dinners, family members coming over, etc.) Promote the heck out of your sale with signage in the hallways, and with students. You have the same issues here as you do with candy of products coming in / going out, and you need to keep careful track of who has taken apples to sell at home / outside of school. Selling during lunch periods only is an easy way to control where everything is.

Peanut apples usually sell best, followed by plain and sprinkled. For every sprinkled apple, I order 2 peanut apples and half a plain apple. So, 500 peanut apples, 250 sprinkled apples, and 125 plain apples is a good start. Do one fundraiser in September, see how it goes, and do another one in November.

The sample order above makes you $350. The apples sell themselves and it's an easy (and fun) 3 day affair! On the third day, if I have enough extra apples, I'll start selling them myself walking through the student cafeteria. Use some slick sales techniques – especially when a guy and a girl are sitting together. Regardless of whether they're actually dating or not, use horrendously out-of date lingo like "Hey guy, why don't you buy one for you and your lady-friend?" The students get a kick out of it. If the guy's actually interested in the girl, or is currently dating her, it gives him a good opportunity to make a purchase. Is that too much sales pressure for high-schoolers? Maybe… but it's all in good fun.

I am usually able to pre-sell about 300 taffy apples to my faculty by the case. A nice e-mail announcement to the faculty and staff is sure to spur sales. (See Chapter 8 for tips on how to write the e-mail.)

Bracelets

If you're doing a charity fundraiser, bracelets are an easy way to turn a profit. They help create awareness for a cause, are easy to sell, and do not spoil / expire.

Let's say that you're raising money to send care packages to your high school alumni that are serving in the military. There are online stores that sell custom bracelets for 19 cents each to 50 cents each. If you were to sell 1,000 bracelets to your faculty, staff, students, and maybe even a few parents at $1 each, you'd clear $810!

These generally work for charities better than anything else – but you could easily have your primary school color as the base, with your club name imprinted on one side.

A colleague of mine sold these easily trying to offset the costs of sending her cheerleader squad to a national competition in Florida. They were able to successfully sell their first order of 1,000 within the school, and set up shop in front of a local grocery store (with the store's permission, of course) to help sell some of the rest. Many people passing by thought it was a cute idea, and anyone that had a young girl with them (the bracelets were light purple), or in their family, stopped to buy one. This very simple fundraiser contributed over $1,500 to their nationals trip.

Travel Mugs

This is a pretty original fundraiser – I don't see too many schools do this, but it's phenomenally easy, especially if your school has never sold them.

Put your school logo, seal, mascot, vision logo, or slogan on a travel mug with your school's name. You can get insulated steel travel (coffee) mugs for under $2 each online, if you buy 100 of them. Sell them for $5 and you've got a pretty instant profit. Some people will buy two or three. I've successfully sold 200 of these in a week – 100 with pre-orders – and the only thing you need to do is advertise, collect money, place the order, and have students help you deliver all the products. There's no product constantly going in and out, so it's real easy to control money and product, unlike candy and taffy apple fundraisers.

A profit of $3 per mug * 200 mugs = $600! Talk about an easy way to make money. The only slight disadvantage is that the travel mugs can take some time to get from the initial order into your hands. Plan ahead – sometimes that's as much as 3 weeks! If you don't have original computer-based artwork for your school's logo (or whatever it is that you're putting on the mug), your principal's office or athletic office can usually help with this, since it needs to go on a lot of official school communications like newsletters and bulletins.

Plush Animals / Oriental Trading Company®

I tried hard not to "plug" any company in this, but I just couldn't resist here. The Oriental Trading Company® product line is just so cheap and sellable that it makes an awesome fundraiser. Last year, for Valentine's Day, I ordered several little stuffed animals for our administration (in appreciation for their support over the school year – which only cost us $12) and they were very well received. Somebody suggested that we sell them to the general student population. So we did! They cost us about $1 each and we sold them for $2 each. We made a dollar per stuffed animal. Both guys and gals gobbled them up, and we even had some faculty members asking us for one. We sold about 150 of them for a quick $150 profit. We didn't do any pre-orders on this one, but could have. In fact, if we had done pre-orders, we probably would've selected something a little bit more expensive and nice (for $1.50) and sold it for $3 or $4.

OTC also has cute things for every event. For example, with the purchase of every plush animal, you could offer a pink or red fortune cookie with a Valentine's Day fortune inside. These say things like, "You'll be getting an e-mail from someone special" or "Hugs are on the way!" The cookies cost about 10 cents each and are a great way to promote the Italian Club, Soccer Team, etc.

Computers

Believe it or not, one of the most lucrative fundraisers we ever did was a computer raffle. You have two options here: You can try to get business partners or local stores to donate a computer, or you can purchase a new one.

You can purchase a very basic laptop or computer for $400 from major manufacturers online with a good sale. Raffle tickets, in my experience, sell best at $1 each, but I know of others that have tried this successfully at $2 each. It depends on your school's population and how much willingness there is for a new laptop. We had some students plunking down $20 for that laptop, because they thought no other student would do the same thing. Faculty and staff were invited to participate. We took all the tickets (more than 1,000 of them) and put them into a pot where an honored guest drew the winner in front of LOTS of people so that nobody could say that it was rigged. (I strongly suggest that you do the same thing.) Selling tickets at $2 each would make $1,600 on this very simple fundraiser. Try getting that kind of number with a bake sale.

So, what do all these "new" fundraisers have in common?

- Uniqueness – every single one of these fundraisers is not something that clubs and organizations do every day. Taffy Apples are probably the most common out of the above items, but they are a unique twist on the traditional candy fundraiser. Find some way of making your fundraiser UNIQUE and it will be successful.

- No real legal issues – you don't have to worry about heat exhaustion, someone getting sick from a bad cake at a bake sale, or anyone getting sunburned. Yes, technology fails, and you might end up with a bad flash drive or two. But, if someone gets a bad flash drive or a leaky travel mug (I've only had ONE case of each in the years that I've been fundraising), then you simply replace the bad product.

- Up-front money – yes, you'll probably have to purchase the raffled computer yourself, if you decide to do that as a fundraiser. Same for the flash drives... but think about the potential profits. $1,600 on a computer raffle is hard to beat. If you time it correctly, you'll only have to carry a balance on a credit card (or have a small dent in the bank account) for a couple of days.

- Quick sales / Guaranteed profits – With the travel mugs, computer, flash drives, plush toys, and even taffy apples, you can take pre-orders. While this is an extra step and a little extra work, you're guaranteed to make your money back. And... all of these things sell quickly because they're unique, relatively cheap, and useful. (Even the plush toys are useful. My principal later told me that she gave the plush animal to her daughter, who refused to sleep without it for weeks. She even brought it to "show and tell" instead of bringing one of her more expensive and interesting toys, much to my principal's amusement.)

So we've covered stuff that we can sell. We've covered places that you can ask for pure, outright donations. What else can you do?

Chapter Six – Other stuff to sell

I always feel somewhat relieved when a product-based fundraiser is over. When the money is deposited into the student activities account and I have a little deposit slip in my hand, I always breathe a small sigh of relief. For the briefest of moments, I promise myself that I won't ever get caught doing another fundraiser like that ever again! But after a few minutes, I realize that our hard work provided invaluable experiences and lessons to the students, and in the process, we're making a few bucks. One day, I realized that you don't actually have to sell a *product* to make money.

Parking spots

This one definitely requires the support of your building administration. Aren't you glad that you got your coalition formed way back in chapter one? Once in a while during the school year, our dean of students will walk around the hallways of the school, passing out raffle tickets to TEACHERS. The first time I got one, I thought he was just being funny. I later learned that you could earn a ticket by simply standing in the hallway during passing period (monitoring students and providing a physical presence that discourages hallway confrontations), picking up a wayward piece of trash, or helping a lost student find their way.

At the end of the week, the dean would draw a raffle ticket and the winner got a "preferred parking spot" that was right next to the building entrance. This worked for the first few months of school, but soon, nobody started paying attention and the dean would have to draw multiple tickets to get a winning number. Teachers were still standing in the hallways, helping students, and doing everything that they always did, but just weren't watching the winning numbers anymore, even if they got the tickets. One of my colleagues from another school had a similar program in place, and asked his administration if he could "lease" the spots for the cold and snowy winter months of December, January, February, and March. Teachers would donate money – $1 per raffle ticket – to be able to park in a preferred spot. It came with a sweet deal: When it snowed during the school day, he would personally go out to that teacher's car and clear off the snow so that the teacher could simply leave work at quitting time.

Talk about a response! In February, a teacher offered a flat fee of $50 to just get the spot. (I personally think she just wanted to have the satisfaction of having him clean off her car.) In warmer climates where it doesn't snow, you could provide "car wash" certificates for a local establishment to go with the parking spot.

Of course, this particular "sale" or raffle really requires you to swallow some pride and show the school (and the rest of the world) that you're willing to go the extra mile to earn every dollar. This group raised at least $100 every month – $400 total – and all the faculty member really had to do was clean off a snowy car once in a while, and the officers of the student organization collected money and sold tickets to the faculty.

Group Specialties

I happen to have extensive experience and training with computer matters. I rounded up some of my highly trained technology students to work on some computers for students, faculty, and staff. As the school's go-to "computer guru," I was always filled with requests for help with upgrading to the latest version of Microsoft Windows® or getting rid of a virus. For a quick donation to the club, we'd gladly assist whoever needed technical help. While we usually used whatever money we made on snacks, it was a fun little business model for a while.

Perhaps that's not your area of expertise... but there's almost always a service that you can provide. Keep looking around the school until you've found one. Choir groups, for example, could deliver "singing telegrams" for $5 each. Art students could draw caricatures during lunch for a small donation. Members of the high school football team could help freshmen carry their stack of textbooks to their lockers during registration week. Figure out what your group's strength is, and use it to provide some kind of service.

Faculty games

Sometimes, you can get enough faculty members (Don't just think basketball coaches and/or P.E. teachers here. Think of teachers that are almost retired, new teachers, everyone...) to go up against each other in a basketball or football tournament *royale*. This works especially best if you have multiple campuses (rivals) within a school district – i.e. "Springfield Central vs. Springfield South."

How does this make money? It depends on how complex you want to get, but through a multi-phase plan of attack, this can make some serious cash. While we *are* actually selling a product *within* the fundraiser (for extra cash), it's not the primary focus of the fundraiser.

The basic idea: Charge admission to a faculty basketball game. Math vs. English, Science vs. Social Studies, or as I said, "Springfield Central vs. Springfield South." Charge $5 admission, and with a mere 200 students attending, you've earned a cool $1,000.

Money can come in through other channels, of course. With almost any sporting event, there are concessions. Popcorn, hot pretzels, small ice cream cups, and even hotdogs and chips are cheap, easy to heat up, and sell well. If each of your 200 students spends $3 at the concession stand, you're looking at an additional $400 profit (after the cost of the concessions). Ask your cafeteria staff (part of your coalition) to donate these items from their stock rooms, if possible. At the very least, ask if they will donate a cheap sack of paper plates and napkins, so that won't come out of your budget.

While T-shirt sales aren't generally a good fundraiser by themselves, they can help you advertise your event. Have students design a spiffy T-shirt and ask your T-shirt company to produce 200 of them at $5 each. Have T-shirts for sale at the door (and through pre-sale), and advertise that for the price of a $10 shirt, admission to the game is free. You've just covered the cost of your T-shirt (which you break even on), still get $5 in admission fees, and you're almost guaranteeing better attendance at the game.

Advertise that there will be a halftime 3 point contest, a race against the school mascot, or other free and FUN events that can generate interest in the game. Have the school's student basketball star(s) go up against the team's basketball coach during halftime.

You can also use this opportunity to sell raffle tickets for any of the above ideas, or a simple split the pot if your school / locality will allow it. Another $100 generated in raffle tickets is a great addition to the night's take.

If done right, this little event should raise at least $1,500 but it does require some planning and effort. At my school, we run a faculty football game during homecoming week with some of these suggestions and easily clear $2,300 after the event is over. We send those profits to a charity, but you can obviously use them for your fundraising objectives. Homecoming week and other well-attended games are easy to use to your advantage. Once you have your school's athletic director on your side (there's that coalition again!), he or she will be able to give you a heads up when the most important events come to town.

Online donations with PayPal

Wait a minute... donations, again? Doesn't this belong in the second chapter?

I suppose it could... But hear me out. This time, you're asking for donations but while offering something in return, and it's a more organized effort that is focused on the faculty and parent groups of your high school.

The basic idea is this: In your town's listening area, there is probably a radio station that depends on public support. Maybe it's the classical radio station, or the public radio station... regardless, these stations don't have traditional audio commercials as top 40 / pop radio stations do. Instead, their main source of revenue comes from listeners offering donations. What's the secret of this? Membership levels.

In return for a donation, the donator becomes an exclusive or honorary member of your club. "For a donation of $10, you get a subscription to our monthly newsletter!" (Have the students write about a recent experience, and e-mail it out so there's no cost in postage.) A donation of $25 gets a copy of the school newspaper mailed to your home, or a mug / pen / USB drive / etc. A donation of $100 gets something really special. You get the idea here. It's an online donation, and you're using the power of the web.

Setting up a PayPal account is pretty easy. It doesn't take a whole lot of web skill to create a "Donate Now" button which links to a PayPal account. If you're unfamiliar with PayPal, it's a way to quickly accept credit card / check donations online. They do charge a very small fee for processing the transaction, but most of that is going towards the credit card company. This is a quick and easy way for people to contribute to your cause. Take, for example, my food drive in chapter three. If I sent an e-mail to my friends, family, fellow faculty members, and others, they could read it at 2:00am and quickly and easily contribute a monetary amount to my cause.

So, are you selling a product here? Kind of. Really, you're selling a membership level to the club. Your actual costs and profit margins depend on what you offer as compensation for the various membership levels. A nice, classy idea that doesn't require a whole lot of work. And if you're not the most technologically advanced teacher on the block, pull your local tech person into your coalition and get them to put something together for you in exchange for a nice dinner or gift certificate!

Silent Auctions

If you've got a lot of parental power, then you can try to run a silent auction or formal fundraiser. This is definitely a huge undertaking, but the rewards are in the thousands of dollars. Your coalition needs to be strong for such an event.

My stepdaughter belonged to a high school choir group that received limited funding for their program. The parents in this group collectively decided to do a banquet with silent auction. The basic day looked like this:

The event would be held at a banquet hall, and lunch would be served. Tickets sold for about $25 and it included lunch and "entertainment" – which consisted of the singing choir group. Before lunch, you could bid on silent auction items that were set up in the back of the banquet hall. Prizes included free trips from local travel agencies, driving lessons (this is high school, after all), parking spots, and product baskets.

To get items for the auction, you'll need to approach the local business side of your coalition. Ask your local Wal-mart, Target, K-mart, and other stores to donate a small item. Sometimes at the end of the day, you'll end up with a variety of items that don't necessarily go together. No problem! Silent auction items can easily be grouped together in baskets to enhance their appeal and value.

For example, let's say that your local Wal-mart donates a coffee maker that's worth $30. Buy a couple of nice travel mugs before you leave the store (or include mugs from a previous fundraiser – see chapter 5) at $5 each, then head to your local Starbucks and purchase a pound of coffee beans for $5. Wrap it all up in a basket from a craft store, and you've got a basket that you spent about $20 on, but is actually worth $50. Since it is a charity event, the minimum bid for the basket starts at, say, $40, and minimum increments are $5 each. The basket will easily net at least $30 profit. Multiply this by 30 baskets and you've got $900.

Think of things to include at little to no cost to you, like parking spots. If you have the school's permission to "auction" off a parking spot, this alone could easily net $200, depending on the parking situation at your school. Trips from a travel agency can net another several hundred dollars, and if you've priced the admission tickets correctly to cover the cost of the banquet lunch, thousands of dollars in profit will result.

I've seen this run successfully for many years. The longer the event is run, the more successful it is. Everyone knows what they need to do, and how to do it.

Think about how you could adjust this event to your group. If you're the sponsor of a sports team, you could feature a multimedia presentation of the team's season with audio, video, and live speeches from students, talking about how the sport has changed their lives. A theater group could easily give performances during the luncheon.

Quite a bit of work? Sure. Do the students have fun and take some financial responsibility for their club? Absolutely. Will it work for you? That depends. I'm sure that you've heard about silent auctions before and that the concept is nothing new to you. I mention the idea here because throughout this book, we're trying to come up with creative ways to adjust a fundraiser to your particular group and fundraising goals. Maybe the whole Saturday luncheon / silent auction / performance thing isn't for you... but you could do an after-work 7:00pm silent auction and hors d'oeuvres fundraiser on a school night while you showcase everything the art students have been working on lately. Perhaps you can have a silent auction added to the faculty basketball game, homecoming agenda, or other event.

My point: As you walk through a typical day, keep your eyes open for things to do and things to sell. Almost *anything* can become a successful fundraiser. It's up to you to figure out what your group's particular needs and goals are, and how you can meet it.

There are some things to stay away from, however. Sometimes the best demonstration of how to be successful is to show people what NOT to do. Let's take a look at some things that I wouldn't include in my fundraising goals.

Chapter Seven – What you shouldn't sell

I've run and seen my share of unsuccessful fundraisers, too. It's only fair to write about some things that haven't worked out, because – well, let's face it. Not everything works out in real life as well as it does in your head. So here are some fundraisers that I've seen or worked with that don't always cut it. Perhaps you'll have better luck with them than I did – but beware of these fundraisers that have significant drawbacks.

Scratch-off cards

The biggest beneficiary here is the company selling you the scratch-off cards. Let me explain what this fundraiser is all about, in case you haven't seen one. You basically buy these "instant scratch-off lottery ticket" cards which have 50-70 "spots" to scratch off. Students take these cards around and ask friends, teachers, and adults to "scratch off" any circle on the card, with the promise to donate that amount of money to their cause. It could be anywhere from 10 cents to $2.00 and the "mystery" or fun in this fundraiser is that the donor has no idea how much they're donating until they scratch off the spots on the cards.

Once every spot is scratched off, all of the donated amounts on each card should total / generate $100 each. The company selling the scratch-off cards charges you $10 each for these cards and claims that you have 90% profit.

Let's say you're fundraising with 50 basketball players... perhaps your Junior Varsity and Varsity squads. 50 players * $10 = $500 to buy the cards. You SHOULD have 50 students * $90 profit = $4,500 profit, but I'll bet that you barely manage to break even with this fundraiser. Here are some secrets that the card companies won't share with you:

- Most of the students, who are doing the selling, will have a hard time convincing their friends (who will do most of the "buying" in any fundraiser) to just donate money to a cause without getting something in return. Re-read the previous chapters, and you'll see that any time my selling focus was the student body, I had a product to offer. Scratch-off companies will tell you to offer a sheet of coupons / deals at local merchants in return for participating, but most students won't respond well to a sheet of coupons. There's no instant gratification.

- If a student was able to ask a teacher to scratch off a couple of spots, and got 60 cents out of the deal, the student had to be able to make exact change. Often, the teachers would just donate a dollar in such a case, but students felt compelled to have exact change on them at all times. Coins aren't really a pleasant thing to carry around, and can be difficult to keep track of.

- As you can imagine, if students have to ask adults to give money, the fundraiser really does take a while to get everyone to scratch off every spot. 2 weeks into the fundraiser, only two students had scratched off all of their spots. This really isn't a good fundraiser if you're looking for a quick turnaround.

- Some students lost the cards after collecting just $5... or they ran into such difficulty that they simply quit asking people after raising their $10 cost. Always having to carry a little lotto ticket with you is harder than the scratch card vendors would have you believe.

Simply put, this is NOT a good fundraiser idea and it has not worked well for me or my colleagues.

"Sponsor me to run laps / shoot free throws."

One day, one of my students on the basketball team approached me after class. "Will you sponsor me to shoot free throws?"

My normal responses followed: "For what? Why are you doing this? What do you have to do?" Part of my incessant questioning is really to find out what his group is up to. In this case, they were subsidizing the cost of new uniforms through a fundraiser.

The other part of me is making him "earn" the donation I'll eventually give him. If you're unfamiliar with this type of fundraiser, a basketball team doesn't really sell anything - but they ask teachers to "sponsor" them at an after-school event where each player will shoot something like 100 free throws. The teacher can donate some amount of money -

either 5 cents per free throw made, or a flat donation. In this example, if my student made 90 out of 100 free throws, I'd have to pay up $4.50. Of course, I'd just rather pay him the $5 even, and have him go on his way.

I didn't think about this type of fundraiser as a "don't do it" event until I discussed it at length with a retired teacher. He remembered that as a swim coach, he would ask students to get sponsors for them to swim laps, and would catch students purposefully collecting donations and not reporting it on their donation sheet, thus pocketing the money. He was insistent that I include it as a topic in this book. There is very little accountability with this fundraiser, and like the previous example, people tend to want something in return when they're giving money for a cause.

Restaurant / Grocery Store Profit Sharing

On the surface, this seems like a really good idea. A local fast food establishment offers to donate 10% of net sales for the evening to whatever your cause happens to be. The key phrase here is NET sales… and once again, you've got to get teachers, family and friends to open up their wallets and pocketbooks to make the fundraiser successful. Timing is key. If you have a fundraiser in late March at a local fast food burger joint, for example, you'll have people not attend your fundraiser night because they're:

- Trying to lose weight for a spring wedding
- Observing lent and are refraining from meat during that time

- On their way home to pick up their son / daughter from childcare before it closes
- Not in the mood for French Fries that night
- Working late, far away, stuck in traffic, etc.

Let's say that you and your group generate $600 in GROSS sales. (I'm calculating that by assuming 60 people attend and spend $10 each, all of them remembering to mention that they're part of the benefit night. That's a lot of happy meals, cheeseburgers, and onion rings.) A restaurant offering to donate 10% of that is only $60... and that's for GROSS sales. Chances are that your organization is only walking away with $40.

Sometimes, you can convince a food establishment to donate all of the net profits, but even then, your profit isn't that high. One group at my high school convinced a fast-food Mexican chain to donate ALL SALES from the fundraiser to their group. The chain offered a deal of $5 for a burrito and soda – and ALL $5 went to the group. If you have 60 people show up and pay $5 each, that's a $300 profit. Getting a chain to go along with such a deal can be hard work, since most establishments will only donate a percentage of that $300. While that will certainly help you reach your goal, the time that you spend advertising the event could easily be put into a more profitable fundraiser.

Need I say more? I think the disadvantage is clear. I wouldn't put the energy into this event unless you're really desperate.

Garage band / talent show night

Basically, this event is where you invite any student that has some kind of musical inclination to showcase his or her skills, or to have garage bands each take 10 minutes on stage. It's a neat idea, and I've heard of a couple of schools do this in an attempt to bring back the whole "Battle of the Bands" thing.

This could turn out really well... or really badly. In my experience as a fundraiser, I haven't seen very good turnout at these events... and this requires a LOT of sound setup, power requirements, lighting, cleanup, etc. If you want to try and make it work, advertise the event around your school and see how many bands you get. Require at least 7 bands to let the event run, since at least 2 of them will cancel sometime before the show / event night.

Notice that this is different from the "Silent Auction" choir fundraiser because of the audience in attendance. Garage band night = student attendance. Choir silent auction and luncheon = student and parent attendance. You might be able to charge $3 - $5 for admission to the event and make it work, but do your research to be sure you'll actually make a profit.

3 on 3 basketball

This is really similar to the "Garage Band" night in terms of what you need for setup. The event involves setting an entrance fee and getting teams signed up and ready to play.

An all-day affair, you can charge each team $20 to enter, and if you have 8 teams sign up to play, that's $160 in the pot... the prize will probably by half of that, so again, you're doing a lot of work for a simple $80 profit. 16 teams generates $320 and $160 of that is your profit... but 16 teams can be a lot to get together. You'll need to have several courts playing simultaneously to be done by mid-afternoon... you'll also need to find fair, impartial referees that will work for free as a charity event, and a water / Gatorade table, at the very least.

All of the events in this section can be summed up with two things: Low profit margins and low participation rates. Those two factors will KILL any chances you have of hitting it big with a successful fundraiser. It's probably better to focus your time and energy on something else.

Again, maybe you've had better experience with one of these fundraisers than I have. And while all fundraisers require hard work, time, and effort, these ways of getting into people's wallets just won't cut it in my book.

Speaking of hard work and effort, it's time to discuss advertising, setup, and other logistics for your fundraiser. On to chapter eight!

Chapter Eight - Logistics

One of the secrets of running a successful fundraiser is delegation.

Delegation can be hard... especially if you've put a lot of hard work and time into your event – from making the first phone calls to making flyers, to taking those hard-earned dollars in to be counted. If you really want to make things easier, I advise you to find a partner that you can trust. Bonnie had Clyde, Santa has Rudolph, and Batman has Robin. Even if you're not good at letting some of the "big stuff" go, little things can help. Find a reliable fundraising buddy (or army of students) to do things like:

Mass mailings

You'll probably want to be the one that writes the letter that you're going to send to local area businesses asking for donations, but students and your partner can do things like:

- Scour the Yellow Pages (either online or in-print) for local businesses and government units to ask for help
- Put the results (accurately) into an Excel spreadsheet file. (And just use a simple Excel sheet. Don't whip up some overly-complex database.)
- Locate and deliver 500 sheets of letterhead and envelopes to your office

- Help fold all the printed letters and stuff them into envelopes
- Sort all of the envelopes by ZIP code for bulk USPS mailing discounts
- Deliver the letters to the postal meter for bulk postage

So here, in a mass mailing fundraising letter, what did you really have to do? Write a letter, get someone to proofread it, set up a mail merge with the Excel spreadsheet, and hit "print." Okay, maybe you helped get business address information by asking your food services department for the local soda / vending machine vendor, and you asked the copy room where your school buys all that paper from – and you even asked the bookstore for the information for your local textbook supplier to see if they'd be a good candidate for helping with your school fundraiser.

But as a whole, sending out simple requests in the mail takes a few hours of work, and can get you several hundred – even several thousand – dollars as a reward. (See chapter two.) If you have a couple of people doing all the running around and "file clerk" work for you, most of this is pretty simple. Just make sure to thank your tech department if they help you with the mail merge or the school's secretary if she helped you stuff envelopes. Things like Starbucks gift cards work really well as thank-you gifts.

Marketing campaign

It's okay if the students make the flyers to be hung around the school for your sale or event. Have the student group that you're raising money for compete against each other for the "3 best fundraiser signs" – the winners get some kind of student reward. Here's a good plan of attack:

1. Give the students the basic information for the event – who, what, where, when, and why, and then set a deadline for the best poster.

2. Let them do the work – and review all of the best posters. Select the top three and duplicate several hundred of them. If your school doesn't charge for / keep track of copies (use your best judgment here), make about a THOUSAND copies in a variety of colors. Then have the STUDENTS post them in the hallways, on random lockers, on classroom doors (get faculty permission or administration permission first!), in the cafeteria at the end of the lunchline, in the bathroom stalls... EVERYWHERE. They know the school as well as, if not better than you. You're not wasting paper (you're really not) but instead ADVERTISING an event. A sign here or there in the hallway might catch a few students' attention, but signs EVERYWHERE will get the students talking, saying to each other as they pass the 17th poster in the last five minutes, "Dang. There must be *something* big going on here. What is this all about?"

Producing the signs takes you a few minutes in the copy room, and you'll need a couple of minutes to get tape and staplers together. Most of the actual work is done by the students – and the more of them you have working for you, the easier this will be. If everyone on your team works together, then this probably takes a grand total of 20 minutes after school if the work is divided up.

Writing the e-mail to your teachers / parents for support

The amount of faculty participation in a school fundraiser can depend greatly on the quality (and timing) of the e-mail that you send them. If your partner is better at this kind of thing, LET THEM DO IT. People can whip through e-mails to filter out the interesting stuff and delete the ever-increasing amount of SPAM in record time. The first step is to actually get your e-mail OPENED by the person on the other end. Let's start there. The first thing to consider when composing an e-mail is the subject line. Which of the following subject lines is more intriguing:

Mugs for Sale

"Those French Club students are at it again!"

Of course, the second one is. Both are appropriate and professional, and you're safe sending the subject to both a teacher's assistant and the superintendent. But only ONE of them will get opened by lots of people. Besides, something like "Mugs for Sale" might even get accidentally deleted as SPAM. How many times have you gotten an e-mail from someone selling prescription drugs or Rolex watches? The phrase, "French Club" provides readers with a little nudge that says, "Hey, listen! This is school-related!" while the phrase "are at it again!" provides just enough of a question to open the e-mail. What are the French Club students doing? Did they get in trouble? Is this something that I should know about?

That momentary question is usually enough for anyone with a hint of curiosity to take a peek. Congratulations, they've opened your e-mail... now, how do you start it?

One approach would be a direct sales pitch. "The French Club is selling Travel Mugs for $5 each. They are blue with a white text lettering and hold 16 oz....."

Again, while that's not technically incorrect, there are probably LOTS of e-mails from faculty and staff that get right to the point. And it's at that point where people will say, "Nope, not interested, delete, move on." We're looking to differentiate your product here. We need to - gulp - SELL IT a little. So how do we do that?

It really depends on the product and the season... and this is something to consider when selling something like travel mugs. You don't want to sell traveler coffee mugs in the summer. Oh sure, people drink coffee in the summer, but GUIDED IMAGERY is so much easier for this particular product in the winter. I sent out my very first e-mail about travel mugs on a Friday afternoon. It was 3:05, and a major snowstorm was about to blanket our area at about 6:00pm. My first lines looked something like:

"With the impending snowstorm, it sure looks like winter will be here for a while. Wouldn't you just love a nice, hot cup of coffee or hot chocolate to take with you on the drive home tonight?

Well, the Springfield Central science club is here to help. We're offering insulated travel mugs..."

I didn't even have the mugs yet -- but I sent it out at just the right time. People were imagining a cold weekend, digging out of several feet of snow (and that's just what it turned out to be) and I played on the image of a nice, piping hot beverage in the midst of all that frigid air. I asked the faculty to e-mail me if they wanted me to "reserve" a mug for them before we sold them to the students. (Sounds classy, doesn't it? I'm not asking for money upfront, nor am I calling it an "order" but rather simply reserving something. As in, "Hey, I'm your buddy. I'll set one aside for you, because I like you.")

By the time I got home at 4:30, I already had orders for 52 mugs! That was more than a quarter of our faculty, and many still hadn't checked their e-mail yet! By the end of the day on Monday, I had pre-sold almost 100 mugs, leaving only 100 more to sell. I asked each club member to sell mugs to family, friends, faculty who didn't pre-order, etc. We sold out in a day and a half. A week later, the mugs arrived ahead of schedule, and we collected and delivered. (When selling to students, it's important to get the money and the order form up front. But that's not important here - we're talking about e-mail to faculty and staff members.)

Again, if you're not the creative type, then don't write the e-mail yourself. Enlist the help of an English teacher or someone on the staff who writes well and has a good sense of humor. Together, the two of you are sure to come up with something clever. Offer this person a free mug in return for his or her help. Done. Great success!

Other things you can delegate

As mentioned before, have someone do things that aren't mission critical. Simple things that advertise your event can eat up lots of YOUR time and energy. Use your coalition to act on your behalf for simple things:

- Press releases are purely optional, but can give you expanded community coverage. Newspapers that serve the district and surrounding communities are always on the look-out for "feel-good" stories that showcase involvement with the local community. If you're not an expert at writing press releases, find someone in your district that has written one before, and submit a release to your local newspaper. If you live in a major metropolitan area, your story might be picked up for print, but odds are against it. You may still get coverage in the online edition of the paper, since it costs much less to publish an article online than in print.

- School marquees are a great (free) way to easily advertise an event like my food drive. We had members of the community see the notice on the electronic sign, and leave canned goods at the main entrance anonymously. Ask whoever is in control of the marquee to publish your event for you. Chances are good that they'll be glad to help.

- Use the student newspaper to help you, if possible. Get the newspaper staff to do a front page article with you. Either ask the newspaper adviser directly or come with free snacks to the next after-school meeting, and ask the students if they would be willing to join your cause.

The day of the event

A few things to think about for the day of your actual event: (Double-check these things a day or two before!) First, be sure that you have a way to capture the event through pictures and/or video. This means making sure that your digital camera battery is charged and has enough space on the card for a hundred pictures, that you have a backup camera somewhere, and that you've got a dedicated photographer for the occasion. This doesn't have to be someone with a degree in photography, but should be someone you trust to take some good close-up pictures of the action. Usually my school's art or yearbook teacher is willing to take good pictures at events. At the very least, trust a good student to do it. It helps greatly if that student is outgoing. He or she need not be the best student in the classroom, but should be able to work a room to get a good shot. That's who you're looking for. Polite, but outgoing.

And don't even THINK about trying to take pictures yourself. You'll be so distracted by what's going on and focused on a good, successful event, that you won't always think to take pictures. If you're really a control freak, have your photographer report to you in the middle of a fundraiser. You can take a minute or two to review the photos and provide further direction and clarification if necessary. As you're reviewing shots, think about pictures that would look good in newsletters, thank-you cards, etc.

D-Day

If you happen to find yourself in a fundraiser where you're depending on both students and third parties for a success (Like selling McDonalds cheeseburgers at lunch, or pizza slices from a local pizzeria), I'd advise you to put a "D-Day" sheet together the night before. It'll make you feel more prepared going into the day. Just keep it in your back pocket, and hope that you never have to pull it out. If you've done your job correctly, everyone will know what to do, where they need to be, and what time it has to happen. Of course, sometimes things don't work out as well in the real world, which is why you need to have this sheet. Things that should be on your sheet include:

- A list of your student workers, and their assigned position for the day (Cashier, garbage cleanup, server, photographer, videographer). Make sure that you assign one student to be your top assistant. They should always be within visual range and have wide knowledge of the school. For example, if you run out of trash bags, you might need to send a trusted student to go and get more from the maintenance department. Pick a student who can leave, and come back in 5 minutes WITH the garbage bags. You don't want someone who will wander around the school or will come back and say "Maintenance is locked" or "Nobody was there."

- A list of critical names and phone numbers, preferably pre-programmed into your cell phone. If you've got a contact at the local pizzeria, get his or her direct line or cell phone so if there is a problem with delivery, you've got a line of communication open. Have the extension of the security desks where the pizza *could* be delivered (for example, have the extension of both the back AND front entrances of the school, even if you've specified delivery to the front entrance 14 times in the last half hour alone). Also have a way to get a hold of the Dean's office / security at your school. If your fundraiser will be off-site (at a Fire station for a carwash, for example), try to have a member of your school administration in your cell phone number. If there's an emergency, you need to have a line of communication open to them.

- If your fundraiser requires a school check (to pay for the cost of the pizzas, for example), make sure that you have that with you. Whenever I do a high-profile fundraiser, I typically have $250 cash in my wallet on that day. I haven't found many problems that $250 can't solve. You never know if you'll need an extra tip for the delivery driver, to send another adult to a trip to a gas station for ice, compensation for dry-cleaning when a student accidentally spilled something on a customer... you name it, and it can happen. This will at least lessen the chances of you freaking out and avoiding disaster.

Chapter Nine – Final Thoughts

After it's over

So your fundraising event is over. First, take a deep breath. After that, don't forget some very important steps.

First, and this seems obvious, but thank everyone for their support. Hopefully, the fundraiser was a success for you and you were able to meet the goal that you set. I usually send three rounds of thank-yous. The first round is an in-person visit or a phone call to your most consistent and generous supporters. This "after the fact" thank-you will encourage those people to donate again during your next fundraiser. As a bonus, you can start next year's phone call with, "I wanted to thank you AGAIN for your support last year, and wanted to know if you'll be able to match last year's donation." Round two is a quick e-mail to your faculty supporters, administration, maintenance, audio-visual, and theater staff. Keep it short, sweet, and to the point.

Round three is a little more involved – but this should be sent to all of your donors, regardless of their donation amount. Take the best five to seven pictures from your event (see chapter 8) and print them *en masse* at your local Wal-mart, Target, Sam's Club, Costco, etc. Send each donor a copy of these pictures (which will only cost about $25 to print, if done correctly) and another short note that includes student quotes from the event, unexpected acts of kindness, or some kind of newspaper article about the event. Be sure to mention that NONE of this would have happened without their support. Once again, even if that $25 comes out of your own personal pocket, you're laying the groundwork for future fundraisers. You'll develop a core group of businesses that are willing to donate, as long as you don't press them too often for funds.

Celebrate success!

All too often, people are hesitant to celebrate success... or it's celebrated improperly. If you had 30 soccer players or 30 students really work their tails off, then it's time to celebrate. Pizza for 30 students really doesn't cost that much, does it? Have a group dinner, kayaking trip, or something that everyone in your group will have fun with. If your event is over, and you've spent considerable time and effort raising funds, take a few moments to savor the victory. Fundraising is not easy work.

Garage Sale

As this book went through a final revision, one of the other staff members at my high school had a brilliant idea. The school year was almost over, and every major club had a fundraiser or two where they sold t-shirts, foam fingers, mugs, tote bags, mousepads, doggie wear, or other school-related paraphernalia. Just about everyone had a few things left over, too. As seniors started to pack up and leave high school, they had one last chance to get "mementos" of their high school experience in a "garage sale" environment.   Gather all the clubs with enough "leftovers" to have a garage sale, and you have a good shot at making some final dollars for summer projects, or as a head start for fundraising for the following school year.

Final Thoughts

Wouldn't it be nice if funding problems just went away? Just ask for funding from your school, and you'd get it?

Part of me says yes – but the "teacher" part of me says that everyone learns something new during a fundraiser. Students learn how much work is actually involved in raising money, and appreciate the end result more than if it were simply paid for them. Faculty and parents get to bond – and there are so many memories when things are over and the dust finally settles.   That's why I recommend having students regularly fundraise for something, even if you work in a school where the families are well-off.

The truth is, most schools are pressed for funds and won't be able to give you the full financial support that you're looking for. I'm so glad that you decided to take matters into your own hands and look for other ways to raise money.   Remember – ANYTHING can be a fundraiser. Always look out for donations, partnership opportunities, and things to sell for a quick profit.

So those are my fundraising secrets. I hope that you've found some new ideas that will be useful to your group. Maybe you've learned that it's important to bring your local government and business partners on board. Maybe you've learned that candy isn't the only thing to sell. Regardless of what you've picked up, I hope that you're coming away from this with a revitalized attitude about getting money for your cause. Remember to build a strong coalition and keep plugging away at your goal. In time, you *will* get there.

Good luck!